The Search Trilogy

A Four-Level Literature
Parent Manual

by Michael Clay Thompson

Royal Fireworks Press
Unionville, New York

October 2017

Royal Fireworks Press
41 First Avenue, P.O. Box 399
Unionville, NY 10988-0399
(845) 726-4444
fax: (845) 726-3824
email: mail@rfwp.com
website: rfwp.com

ISBN: 978-0-89824-818-0

Book designer: Michael Clay Thompson
Cover photo: Dr. T.M. Kemnitz
Publisher: Dr. T.M. Kemnitz
Editors: Jennifer Ault and Rachel Semlyen

Printed and bound in Unionville, New York, on acid-free paper
using vegetable-based inks at the Royal Fireworks facility.

23o17   ps

Table of Contents

Four-Level Literature: General Comments

The purpose of this literature program is to immerse children in great books so that they experience literature as literature and not as a drudgery of tedious school activities. I want children's minds on the books themselves and not on attendant assignments. It is by loving to read that children become literate.

The pedagogy of this program is grown-up and reflective; it is deliberately simple, focusing entirely on the reading of the book and avoiding all traditional worksheet activities in favor of rich discussion and thoughtful writing. Busywork has been eliminated. The activities that are included are flexible options, not a rigid system requiring every step every time. In the end if the child does not love reading, we have failed.

This manual is for the homeschool parent to use in conjunction with the Search Trilogy, which includes *Treasure Island*, *The Call of the Wild*, and *The Invisible Man*. It is called the Search Trilogy because in each novel the main character is plunged into a strange and dangerous situation and has to dig down to deep inner strengths to find a solution. The characters' results in the search are mixed.

The homeschool environment is different in many dimensions from the traditional school environment, and these recommendations take full advantage of the unique flexibility and purity of concentration that occurs in the homeschool setting. In writing a manual for homeschool use, however, I am mindful that the homeschool environment itself exists in many variations. Some children are homeschooled individually, others in small groups or classes. There will be homeschool children using this literature trilogy who are eight or nine years old and others who are of middle school age. There will be homeschool parents who want a grade-free, creative environment and others who want to establish a classical academic rigor that they may feel is lacking in the school system.

My strategy in this manual, therefore, is to provide paths for all of the above. I may refer to the *child*, or I may refer to the *class*, thinking of a small homeschool class. I may provide options for a fifth grader, and I may provide options for a ninth grader, who is by no means too old to read the classics included in the trilogy. Every activity in this manual can be conducted as an ungraded, creative activity, or it can be graded by a parent who wants the child to learn how to navigate a grading system. I do not provide any system for grading.

It is important that the approach to literature be literary, focused on the texts, and simple. I do not want a noisy panorama of activities, worksheets, and other busywork to be the program. The program is the books. I want our approach to be deft and quiet, rather than loud. I want us to behave with literary grace. I want our activities to cuddle up to the books. We will do some creative and academic work in conjunction with the books, with our hearts turned at all times toward the books.

Accordingly, we can think about the program strategy in terms of four simple levels. The four levels are preparing, reading, creative thinking, and writing.

1. Preparing

Prior to reading the book, we might use an encyclopedia or the internet to look up the author and learn about the author's life and the place of the book in cultural history. This content, however, is secondary to the content of the book itself; it would not be important if the book were not important. An alternative is to do this research after reading the book, when the child may be even more curious about the details.

We might also prestudy the vocabulary by studying the words common to all books in the trilogy and then by taking a sneak peak at the words of the novel we are about to read. For the classics in this trilogy, I have provided a list of words common to all three books.

2. Reading

This is the main event. The success of our entire enterprise hangs on this level. We want the reading to be as natural as possible, as uninterrupted as possible, and as magical as possible. We do not want to introduce distractions such as worksheets, objective quizzes, imported systems of interpretation (e.g., symbolism), or literary terms at this stage. Let the child read. Let the story take over. Let there be pirates and wolves and transparent housecats. Trust the author.

It is not the child only who must read. This is not a

program that the parent can assign without also personally reading each book. Read together—even aloud at times. There are no worksheets that can be passed to the child and then graded with an answer key by someone who has not read the story. This program is a magic synergy of book, child, and parent.

I cannot tell you how much to read each day. Pace will vary depending upon your situation. Some children read much faster than others. Thirty pages per day is not unusual, but talented readers often read far more than that—with ease. There are children who love to read an entire book at one sitting, others who would like to read a chapter per day. Set a pace that makes sense, but read complete chapters whenever possible, rather than stopping for the day in the middle of a chapter.

If the child wants to read more than you had planned, wonderful. Let us adjust our processes to celebrate higher achievement.

As the reading progresses, you can monitor with quote quizzes—several quotations that you read aloud— letting the child try to name the character who spoke the words or name the character or events that the words describe. Quotes are pure, are the author's own words. I usually read each quotation two times, and more upon request. The goal is not to catch the child; the goal is to set up a nice, brief talk. I have provided some quotations for you in this manual, but I encourage you to find other good quotes.

I do not like the practice of traditional written quizzes every so many chapters; that is too intrusive. It breaks the continuum of the reading. We should leave the story alone as much as possible. Our pedagogy should tiptoe and whisper.

It is a good idea to have short intratextual discussions about what is happening in the story. Keep it simple; discuss the characters and what they are doing. Ask about their motivations, as if the characters are real people. Keep in mind that even for professional literary critics, the answers to such questions differ. Use Socratic questions, but with a light touch: "Why do you think the character did that?" If the child expresses confusion about what is happening in the story, clarify the question before reading on.

Keep in mind that literature works because the child learns from the characters, not from what we say about the characters. The child must be listening to the character, studying the character's every move, waiting to see what each character does next. The information stream goes from the character to the child, and we want to divert it as little as possible.

At the end of the reading, conduct a complete review of the book, asking about the best parts of the story, the child's favorite character, and what the book seems to be about—the theme or themes. Ask what the book makes one realize.

I like to ask, "If the book is really like the world, is that good news or bad news?" This is not a concrete question. I am not asking whether we still drive buggies. I am asking about human nature. I am asking, if these characters are judging each other on the basis of wealth or social position, is that like the world? The question requires the child to look past the concrete details of technology, clothing, outmoded language, and so forth and assess the deeper elements of character, honor, tragedy, egocentrism, malice, and benevolence.

The exploration of the language illustrations is a culminating activity of the reading stage. After we have completed reading the book and discussing it as a whole from an intratextual point of view, we can go back and discuss the language illustrations. We can linger over them. In each book I have provided close-ups of poetic techniques, four-level analyses of interesting grammar, and comments about writing strategies. These comments all focus on the author's writing technique.

I would like for us to carve out some dedicated time for the illustrations. This should be a thoughtful and relaxed approach, free of anxiety. We want a method that allows enjoyable rereading and thinking back over the illustrations. It cannot be hurried. I have provided a collection of language illustration questions that will help the child to reread and reflect on the illustrations, using questions such as:

1. Which illustration in this section (or book) do you think is most surprising?
2. Which illustration do you think is most important, academically?
3. Which illustration is your favorite?

All three of these questions are positive and are designed to have the child articulate enjoyment or admiration for the writer's technique. If you have a small homeschool class, these questions are ideal for discussion.

The scope of the question, whether it covers one chapter or four chapters at once, is flexible. I do not want to use these questions during the first reading because at that time they would break the spell of the story. These questions about illustrations are extratextual in nature and should be used after the story. They also might provide alternative topics for our writing practices.

3. Creative Thinking

Literature is a high, creative art, and it is not surprisingly a rich ground for creative thinking. I have used many creative approaches to literature, and they always seem to enhance the stories. Be it said: intellectual fun is intellectual. Fun denotes comprehension; you never laugh at what you do not understand. Once, in a traditional school setting, we were reading *The Iliad*, and I had the class perform a five-minute version of the book. The whole story had to be collapsed. Pages got condensed into single words or lines. It was hilarious, but the planning forced the students to think deeply about each section of the book, to decide what to say in the few words that were available.

I have asked students to consider such questions

as, "If you were going to be on a three-day bus trip to another state, who would you rather sit beside?" and give a character from each book. These questions are outside the normal academic line of questioning, but they are catalysts for deep and meaningful thinking and caring about the book. They take the characters seriously. They make the child think about the character as a real individual rather than as a distant fictional entity. I provide some model creative activities and questions, and I encourage you to develop your own.

You will notice that in addition to the creative options that I am including in the creative thinking section, I also have put creative questions in the lists of questions for essays. Look especially for divergent-thinking questions that ask the child to think of more ways, more options, more choices, and so forth. Traditional school questions are convergent, asking the child to find the right answer, but we will feature divergent questions—the exact opposite. Convergent questions focus on what the instructor thinks, but divergent questions are brainstorms; they generate ideas that the child thinks.

---

4. Writing

Literature is the perfect backboard for serious writing practice. In a traditional school setting, writing about books is always graded. In the homeschool setting, this is usually not the case.

Some homeschool parents do not incorporate grades or tests, and some do. The homeschool setting makes it easy for the child to write an essay that is not graded but is discussed. It then can be revised any number of times until it is polished and both child and parent like it. I am not aware of any loss of instructional quality that this entails, compared to a graded situation. At no point does the child need to be told that he or she received a D or a B. You do not make a poor writer better by telling him that you think he is a poor writer. My experience with teaching students to write academic essays shows that the worse the student's writing, the nicer you have to be. You must be honest, but nice about it.

I adamantly oppose deceiving a student by saying that bad writing is good. If it needs work, we must say that it needs work. We can say that there are some problems to work on but that the writing shows promise.

Even though much homeschooling is not graded,

some homeschool parents may wish to incorporate elements of academic rigor that a child eventually will face in higher academics, including grades. That is a choice that you as the parent can make. This literature program does not provide or promote a grading method; my feeling is that students often are overgraded and undertaught. I also would say that I would not wish my own child to arrive at college never before having been graded. You can find some of my thoughts about grading in *Advanced Academic Writing*.

In this program—particularly if a child is of lower elementary age—you may not wish to have formal literature tests, but you may wish to follow reading with writing practice. If you do use tests, then I recommend the steps that follow, and if you do not and would rather just have the child practice writing in a more peaceful context, I would still recommend the steps described in this text; students can write, with or without grades.

I like to ask students to write about a book and to use that writing not only as a way to generate deeper insights into the book but as a way to practice serious academic writing. This writing should follow the completion of the book, rather than interrupt the reading.

I think it is a gross mistake in pedagogy to follow the reading of a wonderful book with a worksheet-style activity containing true/false, matching, multiple-choice, and fill-in-the-blank questions. In my traditional classroom setting, I do not include those or any other form of concrete, objective questions on a literature test. I prefer to deal with plot and character details in discussion. This lets me commit more time to writing practice.

Older students: For children of upper elementary ages and higher, you can assign one or more essays, as described in *Essay Voyage*. In a one-hour space of time, I like for the child to write two essays, and I think that two essays are sufficient. I like to provide four or five thought-provoking study questions several days in advance, and the actual writing practice narrows to three of those questions. One of the three is mandatory, and the child may choose one of the remaining two. By making one question mandatory, I force the child to think about all of the study questions, creating an exceptionally deep exploration of the book. The child therefore writes two essays, and emphasis is on quality. I allow the child to have the book or books in hand in order to quote from the text. I expect quotations to be used as evidence in both essays.

Younger students: For a younger child, talk together about several of the most interesting questions, and decide together which one question would be best or most fun to write about. Even a child who does not yet know what an essay is can write about his or her favorite character or favorite scene. A fourth-grade child can explain which of several books he or she likes best or thinks is most important.

This is academic writing practice, and we must tell the child that practicing the academic style is part of our purpose. We want to practice the conventions of academic writing, of school writing. For older students, these should be formal essays written in academic English with good grammar and punctuation. I expect an introduction, a body, and a conclusion. For younger students, they should at least write what we once called *school writing*. The often-used non-standard English, with first person, contractions, and colloquial expressions, is banished utterly. Even in the creative writing activities, it is better to learn to avoid contractions, and good creative writing is never sloppy.

In addition to no contractions or first person, spelling is important, and a dictionary should be available. Children will benefit from looking words up in the dictionary.

I like to use open-ended interpretive questions, so I do not care as much what the answer is as I do the quality of the English, the structure of the essay, and the quality of the case that the child makes.

The content of the writing practice questions I provide in this manual remains within the internal scope of the story, rather than extending out to the biography of the author or the history of the century or the elements of the literary movement. We may, if we wish, address those things in preliminary research or in subsequent writing. In these essays we are still drilling down into the story. The essays cause the child to reread deeply and to think sensitively about the characters and their lives.

We should avoid rigid formulas and automated steps. Neither good writing nor good teaching is ever robotic. I do not always assign essays at the end of a novel. Usually, however, I do assign essays then. I want the child to reread, rethink, and write with care. I want the child to learn the beauty and power of the essay form. If the child is young and does not yet know what an essay is, this is a perfect moment to begin introducing the idea of an essay with a thesis, an introduction, a body, and a conclusion. A nine-year-old can certainly begin learning that.

In the spirit of what you have seen in *Sentence Island*, *Paragraph Town*, and *Essay Voyage*, my instructions to the older student include that each essay:

1. Must be a true essay with an introduction, a body, and a conclusion that ties the argument together. The essay must have a thesis. In other words, it cannot be a retelling of the plot; it must present an idea. There must be proper paragraphing. The standard teaching model for the essay is a five-paragraph model, but this is only a beginner's model. Real essays usually have more paragraphs than five.

2. Must be in standard English with correct spelling and punctuation. The style must be academic with no contractions and no first person. By forbidding first person, we force the child to write directly about the content itself.

3. Must contain short and long quotations that

provide evidence and make a case. We want a text-based interpretation, not a spontaneous opinion.

To give you some idea of what I expect students to write, I provide a sample essay on the following pages about an invented book. If you have seen my *Advanced Academic Writing* text, you will note that the essay resembles a handwritten MLA paper; we want to seize every possible opportunity to give the child practice in writing academic English.

For a younger child, we need not mention MLA; we simply can use the sample essay as a model and ask the child to imitate it. This writing practice can be used beautifully in conjunction with *Paragraph Town* and *Essay Voyage*; both of those books provide recommendations and instructions for how to write such assignments. We also might use some of the questions that I have provided as the basis of good discussions rather than of writing practice.

2. Why does Mildred Moose distrust Mango the Mongoose?

In James Merriwether's novel, *The Spruce Moose*, Mildred Moose comes to distrust Mango the Mongoose, and she does this for good reason. Mango repeats what she tells him in confidence, he eats grass from her swamp when she is not looking, and he pretends to be her friend even though he tells other animals he is not.

At the beginning of the story, Mildred approaches Mango in the forest and asks him for help. She says that she is "in some confusion" (Merriwether 25) about where the swamp is because she has gotten lost. Mango pretends to be concerned: "Poor thing. Let me help you get back to the swamp. I know you must be hungry by now, for the sun is hot, and there is no breeze" (27). As they make their way through the forest, Mildred tells Mango about the mistakes she has made that got her lost, and she makes him promise not to tell anyone. Mango agrees, but the following day, Esquire Squirrel chirps from the treetop: "Hee chee chee, Mildred! You couldn't find your way out of a footprint!" (32).

Mildred knows that Mango told Esquire Squirrel what happened, and her feelings are hurt by Mango's betrayal of her confidence, but she decides that Mango did not mean to reveal her confusions. She forgives Mango, and the next morning she makes her way down her usual path to the swamp, hungry for sweet swamp grass. When she gets to the swamp, she is shocked at what she sees:

> Across the swamp there was a mongoose party. Seventeen mongooses were nibbling tender grass shoots, rolling in the long grass and crushing it, laughing about what the foolish moose would say. Mango was the loudest mongoose in the picnic, showing his friends where the best grass was and telling them to hurry before Mildred arrived. (41)

Looking in disbelief at the mongooses spoiling her swamp, Mildred was hurt. She stepped out of the shadows of the trees and "moofed" (42) in her loudest voice. All mongooses vanished in a split second, leaving *"nothing but ripples in the water" (43).*

Later that day, Mango came to see Mildred. He said that he wanted "to explain what he was trying to do for her" (47) and that animal activity was the best way "to make swamp grass grow tall and green" (48). He promised that she would see the grass grow.

By this time Mildred had come to understand Mango more clearly, and she realized that he was trying to deceive her. He had broken her confidence by talking to Esquire Squirrel, he and his friends had eaten the new grass she was so looking forward to, and he had lied about being her friend. Before she fell asleep that night, she curled her hooves up in a comfortable way and thought, "Mango, tomorrow I will have a surprise for you. You have messed with the wrong moose" (62).

Work Cited

Merriwether, James. The Spruce Moose. Boston: Smith, 1997.

Notice in this sample how short and long quotations are treated. Long quotations of more than four lines are indented. Short quotations have quotation marks around them. All quotations are documented with page numbers, and the first documentation also has the book author's name. The essay has an introduction, a body organized into logical paragraphs, and a conclusion that ties everything together. There is no first person, and there are no contractions.

MLA Papers for Older Students

For younger children the writing practice should take place at an introductory level; the child may be just learning about paragraphs or just beginning to learn what an essay is.

On the other hand, some children already might feel comfortable with paragraphing and with an essay having an introduction, body, and conclusion. A child may be ready to learn to research a subject and to write about it in a more formal way.

If the child is older and ready for more than a simple essay, we might assign a short, typed MLA paper that requires either an interpretation of the theme of the book or a comparison of two or more books we have read. It is not unusual to see students in fifth or sixth grade writing introductory-level MLA papers. The full instructions for this type of paper appear in the *Advanced Academic Writing* program.

The MLA paper is an excellent opportunity to let the child step back from the book and research the place of the book in intellectual history. It is also an excellent opportunity to learn to look up something in a library.

As you will see from the *Advanced Academic Writing*

text, MLA is the most widely used research paper format in the world. It is powerful but simple. It gives students practice in all elements of formal language study. They must do library research and read copious academic nonfiction. They must write in correct grammar, in complete sentences, in clear paragraphs, with a thesis, using quotations, without first person or contractions, with correct punctuation, using academic vocabulary, without wordy modifiers, and with attention to a good idea about literature, not to mention the things I have not mentioned.

I have learned that the secret to teaching children to write high-level academic papers is to write short papers repeatedly, placing emphasis entirely on quality instead of quantity.

FOUR-LEVEL LITERATURE

1. PREPARING
2. READING
3. CREATIVE THINKING
4. WRITING

Search Trilogy Vocabulary Prestudy

Here are six words that appear in all three novels. Let us examine them before beginning the trilogy.

apprehension: n.
apprehensive: adj.
apprehensively: adv.

Apprehension is a fear about what might happen, as when Jack London wrote that "Buck watched them apprehensively" or when H.G. Wells wrote that "His mottled face was apprehensive." Robert Louis Stevenson wrote of "the worst of my apprehension realised."

In *The Prince and the Pauper*, Mark Twain wrote that there was "a touch of nervous apprehension in his voice," and Charles Dickens wrote in *Great Expectations* that "I was in an agony of apprehension."

There is a second meaning in which *apprehension* is an understanding, a mental grasp of the situation, as when Wells describes one character as "a man of sluggish apprehension."

diabolical or **diabolic**: adj.
diabolically: adv.

From the Latin *diabolus*, *diabolical* means devilish. Jack London described "eyes diabolically gleaming," and H.G. Wells wrote that the "man must have had diabolically acute hearing." Robert Louis Stevenson wrote that "I would see him in a thousand forms, and with a thousand diabolical expressions." In Emily Brontë's *Wuthering Heights*, we read that "Mr. Heathcliff dislikes me; and is a most diabolical man, delighting to wrong and ruin those he hates, if they give him the slightest opportunity." In *Dracula*, Bram Stoker wrote that "He smiled, such a soft, smooth, diabolical smile that I knew there was some trick behind his smoothness."

Modern writers have continued to use *diabolical* to describe evil or the appearance of evil. In *The Crucible*, Arthur Miller described "diabolical malevolence," and in Arthur Conan Doyle's *The Hound of the Baskervilles*, we read that "there is a diabolical agency which makes Dartmoor an unsafe abode for a Baskerville." Maya Angelou used *diabolic*, a variant, in *I Know Why the Caged Bird Sings*: "He seemed positively diabolic in his enjoyment of our discomfort."

meditation: n.
meditative: adj.
meditate: v.

To meditate is to think profoundly, to focus one's thoughts on something for an extended period, often silently. In Wells's *The Invisible Man*, "His meditation became profound," and "He remained meditative for a space after doing this." In *Treasure Island*, Stevenson wrote that "I had seen him meditating a fresh treachery." In *The Call of the Wild*, Jack London wrote that "He was friendly, in a treacherous sort of way, smiling into one's face while he meditated some underhand trick, as, for instance, when he stole from Buck's food at the first meal."

In *Great Expectations*, Dickens described "Joe, pausing in his meditative raking of the fire," and in Mark Twain's *The Prince and the Pauper*, we read that "He was soon deep in meditation." Harper Lee gave us one of the most humorous examples in *To Kill a Mockingbird*: "she spat meditatively into the yard."

perplexity: n.

perplex: v.

perplexed: adj. or v.

The English noun *perplexity* comes from the Latin *perplexus*, entangled. When something is so complicated or opaque that it baffles us, we are perplexed. In Jack London's *The Call of the Wild*, "The driver was perplexed." In *Treasure Island*, Robert Louis Stevenson wrote that "At last, with a swallow or two, he spoke, his face still wearing the same expression of extreme perplexity."

H.G. Wells used variations of *perplexity* repeatedly in *The Invisible Man*, writing that "her face was eloquent of her surprise and perplexity," describing "sounds within distinct and perplexing," and noting that "He stared at it in infinite perplexity." Most vividly, Wells described "a little group of a dozen people perhaps, studying with infinite perplexity a slowly drying footprint that had resulted from a puddle in Tavistock Square, a footprint as isolated and incomprehensible to them as Crusoe's solitary discovery."

resolution: n.

resolute: adj.

resolutely: adv.

To be resolute is to act with great purpose and determination, without hesitation or waver. The opposite form of the word is *irresolute*. In Jack London's *The Call of the Wild*, "He took all manner of risks, resolutely thrusting his little weazened face into the frost and struggling on." In *Treasure Island*, we read, "As soon as I remembered I was not defenceless, courage glowed again in my heart and I set my face resolutely for this man of the island and walked briskly towards him."

H.G. Wells used the word often in *The Invisible Man*, writing that "She went to these things resolutely," that "she was a resolute woman," that the "face of Mr. Cuss was angry and resolute," and that he "attacked his work resolutely."

One of the immortal uses of *resolute* comes from William Shakespeare's *Macbeth.* In Act IV, scene i, the Second Apparition says to Macbeth: "Be bloody, bold, and resolute; laugh to scorn / The power of man, for none of woman born / Shall harm Macbeth."

---

writhe: v.

writhing: adj.

To writhe is to twist, squirm, or contort one's body in agony or for another reason. The word is of Germanic origin and is related to the idea of wreathing, of intertwining. In *Treasure Island*, "Israel Hands turned partly round and with a low moan writhed himself back to the position in which I had seen him first." In *The Call of the Wild*, "Joe whirled around on his heels to face him, mane bristling, ears laid back, lips writhing and snarling." London repeatedly described the angry dogs' lips as writhing, but he also applied the word to muscles: "His whole body was gathered compactly together in the tremendous effort, the muscles writhing and knotting like live things under the silky fur." H.G. Wells used the past tense of the verb form in *The Invisible Man*: "Adye writhed, raised himself on one arm, fell forward, and lay still."

Mary Shelley used *writhe* poignantly in *Frankenstein*: "I writhed under his words, yet dared not exhibit the pain I felt," and "I now writhed under the miserable pain of a wound."

STRATEGIES AND ACTIVITIES

For each title in this trilogy,
you will find:

1. A Comment

2. Language Illustration Questions

3. Character Quotations for Quote Quizzes

4. Creative Questions and Activities

5. Academic Writing Practice

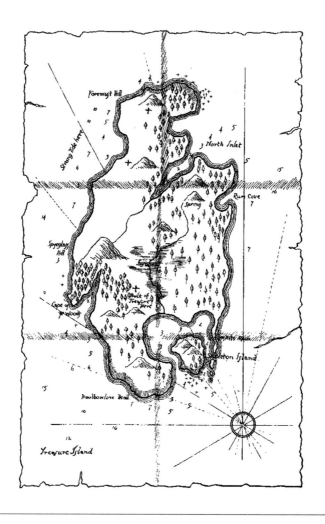

Treasure Island

A Comment

If you think about the matter objectively, you might not conclude that Robert Louis Stevenson's *Treasure Island* actually is what many books only claim to be: unforgettable. After all, its good-guy-bad-guy plot is predictable. From the first paragraph of the novel, you know that it will have a happy ending. You never worry that narrator Jim Hawkins will be killed, or that Long John will win in the end, or that the book will spiral into ghastly tragedy. Furthermore, many of Stevenson's characters are even likeable; how shallow.

In *Treasure Island* the good guys are good, though sometimes obtuse (think Squire Trelawney), and the bad guys, though they may dissemble their malevolence or moral indifference, are bad. No one is redeemed, no one changes, no important character switches sides. There are no moral dilemmas. It is flat good versus flat bad—like *Star Wars* on a boat.

There is also not the inconvenient complexity of character that you find in Jane Austen or Charles Dickens. There are not troubling dimensions to the personalities. The characters are a bit like J.M. Barrie's Tinker Bell, who was so little that she could have only one emotion at a time; they never seem to be in conflict with themselves. Even the slightly conflicted, ambivalent relationship between Jim and Long John does not seem deeply troubled.

On cursory inspection, *Treasure Island* seems conceptually elementary. You do not feel threatened by deep meanings or subtle observations about reality. The narrative exposes no discouraging disclosures, no philosophical disappointments, no perplexities, no criticisms of conventional mores. When you finish reading *Treasure Island*, you do not even feel worse about yourself.

How *unmodern*.

Joseph Campbell taught us the structure of the mythical hero's quest: to leave the safety of what you know and to journey out into an unknown place where you encounter a danger for which you are not prepared. By trusting your inner truth, you overcome the challenge and return home with new enlightenment.

Jim Hawkins does not do that.

Jim Hawkins does go to a dangerous and mysterious world, but he more experiences it than reflects upon it. He survives it, not because he changes but because he does not. His struggles with the perils of Treasure Island—and with the peril of Long John Silver in particular—seem merely to confirm his inner character, not build it or clarify it. In the end Jim simply does what the doctor and the squire ask him to do—he writes down the particulars of their adventure, which, even years later, he does not seem to have reevaluated.

Yes, Long John is a magnetic character, a diabolical charmer. Long John reminds us of Shakespeare's frightening Iago in *Othello*, an evil genius—the sort that today we would call a sociopath, a predatory manipulator who is utterly convincing to his doomed victim. Yet can we imagine Long John carrying through the plot that Iago completes, of deceiving good Othello into murdering his good wife Desdemona? I think not. For all of his deceit, Long John is no Iago. Iago would deceive even Long John. The serene Iago might be the most terrifying character in all of literature, but Long

John, for all of his oleaginous villainy, is not terrifying. Long John is captivating; at times he is almost a cartoon.

No, *Treasure Island* is no *Othello*. For all of its villains, it is not tenebrous; it is luminous. It is an inevitable triumph of good, confirming our hopes. It is the cowboys and the pirates.

If we think about the matter objectively, we might almost conclude that *Treasure Island* is a classic by mistake, that it is pretty but dismissible, a tall story of little consequence.

The problem with dismissing it, of course, is that despite any critical attempt to dissect the flaws of *Treasure Island* with intellectual instruments, the book mysteriously lingers in one's fondness, even decades after reading it. If there are flaws in the book, we love it anyway. There is a genius in *Treasure Island*, even if it is not dreamt of in our critical philosophies, that causes the book to be reprinted and reread—and re-illustrated by our greatest illustrators such as N.C. Wyeth—long after its first printing in 1883.

Paradoxically, the very simplicities that are the putative weaknesses of the novel are its strengths. *Treasure Island* is, above all else, a stupendous story. It is not pallid with doubt or languid with ambiguity. It is not conflicted. It is a primary-color masterpiece of adventure imagination. The scary guys in *Treasure Island* have dirty, livid sabre cuts across their cheeks, for Pete's sake. The pensive, cautious, ambiguous, and self-doubting wounds of modern fiction that *Treasure Island* lacks would be detriments to the speed and the imagination of this story. Its characters are clear, intelligible, and sometimes heroic. Its dangers are dangerous. Its morals are visible and are the cultural morals one brings to the book before reading it. It has traps and triumphs, victories and villainies, sounds and sights and scenes. It leaps at you. It is no book for sissies.

You read *Treasure Island*, and for the rest of your life you hear the feathered Cap'n Flint squawking "Pieces of eight!" You hear, chronically, the blue rollers booming on the reef, and you watch Israel Hands eternally splashing into the sea, as though he were tied to a great invisible wheel in the mind: turn-splash, turn-splash. Years later, you still hear Billy Bones roaring at the Admiral Benbow inn, inexorably, like a grandfather clock. You hear Long John's crutch stomping somewhere in the next room. You freeze.

Treasure Island is not a novel that makes you think. It makes you experience. It takes you somewhere and makes you like it. It plunges you into a voyage so vivid that part of you never returns from the island; there you remain, sunburned and salt-crusted, with the palm fronds whishing in the on-shore wind. Stevenson accomplishes this not only through brilliant description of detail but also through brilliant crafting of language, contrasting the logical, erudite words and syntax of Jim Hawkins and Dr. Livesey with the salty maritime argot of John Silver and his brackish pirates.

Of course, the idea-level in *Treasure Island* is not zero. I do not mean to be too absolute, for the book is not stupid. It is not vacuous. It is a book of genius, and Stevenson does occasionally let the wink of an idea peer through a crack in the pell-mell. One of my favorite moments is in Chapters 28 and 29 when the pirates rise against Long John's leadership. Here we have a band of dissolute cutthroats as villainous as ever may be feared, who think nothing of mutiny, murder, and treachery, and yet they are locked in a dainty debate about the rules of leadership and the decorous procedures for deposing Long John. The stubbled pirates are fastidious about pirate rules, and each pirate feels bound by the pirate rules of order. Long John uses pirate parliamentary procedure to outmaneuver his fellow rogues. It is too wonderful. You could not make this stuff up. Oh, wait, Stevenson did make it up.

The best relationship in the book is between Jim Hawkins and Long John Silver. For all of its twists, and for all of Long John's treacherous sangfroid, there is a mutual wink between the two. Heaven help them, they like each other, even as they mistrust and scheme against one another. They are, to make a preposterous comparison, a bit like Romeo and Juliet; they are the two smartest people on the boat; they recognize each other, and they connect through the electricity of each other's crackerjack intelligence. Jim perceives and enjoys the chess moves of John's duplicities, and John knows that Jim really is, as John says, "as smart as paint." When John tells Jim that "I have always liked you, for a lad of spirit," we believe him. John's pretenses about saving Jim's life and his loyalty to Jim are both lies and truths; he and Jim both know that they are lies, but John feels them anyway. The cleverness of this relationship is bewitching. You watch these two with your nose in the book, leaning forward, unaware of the pages you turn. Unaware that pages exist.

Relationships alone, though, do not explain *Treasure Island*'s hold on our affection. The more you think about this hold, the more you notice the language of the novel, and particularly the pirate language. It is the pirate language that is extraordinary. We hear people speaking more or less like Jim Hawkins all the time, but we have never heard anyone speaking like Long John. No one of our acquaintance, when asking us to come closer, says we should "come alongside" or, when wanting us to get away, cries "Avast!" No one, when asking for quiet, bellows "Silence, there, between decks!" No one calls us *lubbers*.

Imagine a near-identical book, with mirror characters and mirror plot structures, but a book in which the bad guys were all social and educational twins of Jim and Dr. Livesey. Imagine that the polar contrast between Hawkins-language and Silver-language was negated and that Long John spoke well. What then? Would the book still seep into our bones the way it does? No, much of the magic of the book is in Stevenson's construction of the pirates, not just their evil intentions and treachery but their piratey jabber.

Consider, for example, this passage that demonstrates both Jim's and Long John's language. Jim narrates:

> In any other circumstances it would have been comical to see his slow advance, hesitating as he set down each foot, but holding his closed right hand in front of him.
>
> "Step up, lad," cried Silver. "I won't eat you. Hand it over, lubber. I know the rules, I do; I won't hurt a depytation."

What if Long John Silver's portion of the passage read this way:

> "Approach, young man," said Silver. "You are safe with me. Give that to me, please, seaman. I am cognizant of the expected procedures; I would never do harm to any deputation."

It is not that the book then would have no chance at greatness; after all, Jane Austen's novels are populated by refined characters whose grammar, diction, and verbal courtesy are eloquent. And yet if everyone in *Treasure Island* spoke like Jim Hawkins, the book would be a linguistic flat earth, a uni-locus. The fun of contrast would be deflated, and the element of the book that most required Stevenson's imagination would be gone. No, we would not want the book to teem with college types. *Treasure Island* is no place for accountants; there must be parrots, livid scars, and clumping sea-cooks.

There must be lies.

Years later, long after you have closed the cover, it is not the voice of Livesey that you hear. It is that pirate parrot, Cap'n Flint, squawking into the jungle "Pieces of eight!" and "Stand by to go about!" and the crude growl of Billy Bones shouting "Silence between decks" and singing about fifteen men on the dead man's chest, and Long John himself addressing his crew:

> "There was some that was feared of Pew, and some that was feared of Flint; but Flint his own self was feared of me."

I am feared of him. Even now.

Treasure Island

Language Illustration Questions

The following questions concern the language illustrations that appear in this edition of Robert Louis Stevenson's *Treasure Island*. These questions will promote a thoughtful involvement with what the illustrations reveal about Stevenson's writing.

1.   In Part One of the novel, Chapters 1-6, which three language illustrations were most surprising to you? Why?

2.   Which of the language illustrations in Part Two, Chapters 7-12, taught you most about writing?

3.   What do you think is the point of the language illustration on page 164? Explain.

4. Please explain the point of the language illustration on page 189. Then explain the language illustration on page 207. Which of these two is your favorite? Why?

5. What do you learn about writing from the language illustration on page 240?

6. Please explain the technique shown in the language illustration on page 275. Then explain the language illustration on page 287. Which illustration taught you more?

7. Which three language illustrations in Part Six, Chapters 28-34, do you like best? Explain.

Treasure Island

Character Quotations for Quote Quizzes

Here are quotations that may be used for quote quizzes. I will not provide any certain number per chapter; you may select from them as seems appropriate. I have adjusted capitalization and other details slightly for formatting purposes, but I have not changed any words. Each quotation begins with the number of the chapter in which it is found. I encourage you to use these as models and to enjoy finding more. In practice I did not give quote quizzes every day; when I did give one, I used three to five quotes, reading each one carefully two times. All the students had to do was to write the name of the character whose words they were.

Notice that the quotations are always the words of a character, never the words of the narrator. If you want to choose some of your own quotations, here are some tips: find quotations that are famous, that have clues in them such as grammar or ways of speaking unique to a character, that are memorable or repeated, that mention plot details that give them away, or that reveal important aspects of a character's personality. Try to find quotations that should be obvious to any child who really has read the story, not quotations that are subtle, tricky, or overly challenging. We do not want the quote quizzes to be dreaded. Here are some *Treasure Island* quotes that you might like to use:

1. I remember him as if it were yesterday, as he came plodding to the inn door, his sea-chest following behind him in a hand-barrow. - Jim

1. I'm a plain man; rum and bacon and eggs is what I want, and that head up there for to watch ships off. What you mought call me? You mought call me captain. - Billy Bones

1. Were you addressing me, sir? I have only one thing to say to you, sir, that if you keep on drinking rum, the world will soon be quit of a very dirty scoundrel! - Dr. Livesey

---

1. If you do not put that knife this instant in your pocket, I promise, upon my honour, you shall hang at the next assizes. - Dr. Livesey

2. Is this here table for my mate Bill? - Black Dog

2. Now, look here, you've run me down; here I am; well, then, speak up; what is it? - Billy Bones

2. I was quite unsteadied by all that had fallen out, and I broke one glass and fouled the tap, and while I was still getting in my own way, I heard a loud fall in the parlour. - Jim

2. You have been drinking rum; you have had a stroke, precisely as I told you; and I have just, very much against my own will, dragged you headforemost out of the grave. - Dr. Livesey

3. Doctors is all swabs, and that doctor there, why, what do he know about seafaring men?
- Billy Bones

3.   I want none of your money but what you owe my father. I'll get you one glass, and no more. - Jim

3.   I was first mate, I was, old Flint's first mate, and I'm the on'y one as knows the place. He gave it me at Savannah, when he lay a-dying, like as if I was to now, you see. - Billy Bones

3.   Business is business. Hold out your left hand. Boy, take his left hand by the wrist and bring it near to my right. - Blind Pew

3.   As soon as I saw that he was dead, I burst into a flood of tears. It was the second death I had known, and the sorrow of the first was still fresh in my heart. - Jim

4.   If none of the rest of you dare, Jim and I dare. Back we will go, the way we came, and small thanks to you big, hulking, chicken-hearted men.
     - Mrs. Hawkins, Jim's mother

---

4. Then my mother got a candle in the bar, and holding each other's hands, we advanced into the parlour. He lay as we had left him, on his back. - Jim

4. Overcoming a strong repugnance, I tore open his shirt at the neck, and there, sure enough, hanging to a bit of tarry string, which I cut with his own gully, we found the key. - Jim

5. Down with the door! - Blind Pew

5. It's these people of the inn—it's that boy. I wish I had put his eyes out! - Blind Pew

5. In fact, sir, I believe I have the thing in my breast pocket; and to tell you the truth, I should like to get it put in safety. - Jim

6. Mr. Dance, you are a very noble fellow. And as for riding down that black, atrocious miscreant, I regard it as an act of virtue, sir, like stamping on a cockroach. - Squire Trelawney

6. Heard of him, you say! He was the blood-thirstiest buccaneer that sailed. Blackbeard was a child to Flint. - Squire Trelawney

6. But you are so confoundedly hot-headed and exclamatory that I cannot get a word in.
   - Dr. Livesey

6. The squire and I were both peering over his shoulder as he opened it, for Dr. Livesey had kindly motioned me to come round from the side-table.
   - Jim

6. Hawkins shall come as cabin-boy. You'll make a famous cabin-boy, Hawkins. You, Livesey, are ship's doctor; I am admiral. - Squire Trelawney

7. The admirable fellow literally slaved in my interest, and so, I may say, did everyone in Bristol, as soon as they got wind of the port we sailed for—treasure, I mean. - Squire Trelawney

7. I said good-bye to Mother and the cove where I had lived since I was born, and the dear old Admiral Benbow. - Jim

8. I had seen the captain, and Black Dog, and the blind man, Pew, and I thought I knew what a buccaneer was like—a very different creature, according to me, from this clean and pleasant-tempered landlord. - Jim

8. If he were Admiral Hawke he shall pay his score. Who did you say he was? Black what? - Long John

8. You're a lad, you are, but you're as smart as paint. I see that when you first come in. - Long John

8. Dooty is dooty, messmates. I'll put on my old cockerel hat, and step along of you to Cap'n Trelawney, and report this here affair. - Long John

9. Well, sir, better speak plain, I believe, even at the risk of offence. I don't like this cruise; I don't like the men; and I don't like my officer. That's short and sweet. - Captain Smollett

9. Well, gentlemen, I don't know who has this map; but I make it a point, it shall be kept secret even from me and Mr. Arrow. Otherwise I would ask you to let me resign. - Captain Smollett

9. Contrary to all my notions, I believe you have managed to get two honest men on board with you—that man and John Silver. - Dr. Livesey

10. Mr. Arrow, first of all, turned out even worse than the captain had feared. He had no command among the men. - Jim

10. Nobody more welcome than yourself, my son. Sit you down and hear the news. Here's Cap'n Flint—I calls my parrot Cap'n Flint, after the famous buccaneer—here's Cap'n Flint predicting success to our v'yage. - Long John

10. A trifle more of that man, and I shall explode. - Squire Trelawney

---

10. Now, just after sundown, when all my work was over and I was on my way to my berth, it occurred to me that I should like an apple. - Jim

11. Flint was cap'n; I was quartermaster, along of my timber leg. The same broadside I lost my leg, old Pew lost his deadlights. - Long John

11. You look here: you're young, you are, but you're as smart as paint. I see that when I set my eyes on you, and I'll talk to you like a man. - Long John

11. There was some that was feared of Pew, and some that was feared of Flint; but Flint his own self was feared of me. - Long John

11. You may fancy the terror I was in! I should have leaped out and run for it if I had found the strength, but my limbs and heart alike misgave me. - Jim

12. I have, sir. I've watered there with a trader I was cook in. - Long John

12. Doctor, let me speak. Get the captain and squire down to the cabin, and then make some pretence to send for me. I have terrible news. - Jim

12. You, sir, are the captain. It is for you to speak. - Squire Trelawney

13. If the conduct of the men had been alarming in the boat, it became truly threatening when they had come aboard. They lay about the deck growling together in talk. The slightest order was received with a black look and grudgingly and carelessly obeyed. - Jim

13. Silver, sir, he's as anxious as you and I to smother things up. This is a tiff; he'd soon talk 'em out of it if he had the chance, and what I propose to do is to give him the chance. Let's allow the men an afternoon ashore. - Captain Smollett

14. I now felt for the first time the joy of exploration. The isle was uninhabited; my shipmates I had left behind, and nothing lived in front of me but dumb brutes and fowls. - Jim

14. Mate, it's because I thinks gold dust of you—gold dust, and you may lay to that! If I hadn't took to you like pitch, do you think I'd have been here a-warning of you? - Long John

14. And as for you, John Silver, long you've been a mate of mine, but you're mate of mine no more. If I die like a dog, I'll die in my dooty. - Tom

15. I began to recall what I had heard of cannibals. I was within an ace of calling for help. But the mere fact that he was a man, however wild, had somewhat reassured me. - Jim

15. You mightn't happen to have a piece of cheese about you, now? No? Well, many's the long night I've dreamed of cheese—toasted, mostly—and woke up again, and here I were. - Ben Gunn

---

15. It's not Flint's ship, and Flint is dead; but I'll tell you true, as you ask me—there are some of Flint's hands aboard; worse luck for the rest of us. - Jim

15. Well, there's my boat, that I made with my two hands. I keep her under the white rock.
    - Ben Gunn

16. It never occurred to us to doubt Jim Hawkins, but we were alarmed for his safety. With the men in the temper they were in, it seemed an even chance if we should see the lad again. - Dr. Livesey

16. Gray, I am leaving this ship, and I order you to follow your captain. - Captain Smollett

17. At any rate, the boat sank by the stern, quite gently, in three feet of water, leaving the captain and myself, facing each other, on our feet. - Dr. Livesey

18. Captain, Trelawney is the dead shot. Give him your gun; his own is useless. - Dr. Livesey

---

18. Dr. Livesey, in how many weeks do you and squire expect the consort? - Captain Smollett

18. Captain, the house is quite invisible from the ship. It must be the flag they are aiming at. Would it not be wiser to take it in? - Squire Trelawney

19. Well, I believe I understand. You have something to propose, and you wish to see the squire or the doctor, and you're to be found where I found you. Is that all? - Jim

19. That man Smollett is a better man than I am. And when I say that it means a deal, Jim. - Dr. Livesey

19. First ship that ever I lost. - Captain Smollett

20. Cap'n Silver! Don't know him. Who's he? - Captain Smollett

20. Why, Silver, if you had pleased to be an honest man, you might have been sitting in your galley. It's your own doing. You're either my ship's cook—and then you were treated handsome—or Cap'n Silver, a common mutineer and pirate, and then you can go hang! - Captain Smollett

20. Well, here it is. We want that treasure, and we'll have it—that's our point! You would just as soon save your lives, I reckon; and that's yours. You have a chart, haven't you? - Long John

20. Now you'll hear me. If you'll come up one by one, unarmed, I'll engage to clap you all in irons and take you home to a fair trial in England.
- Captain Smollett

21. Doctor, you will take the door. See, and don't expose yourself; keep within, and fire through the porch. Hunter, take the east side, there. Joyce, you stand by the west, my man. - Captain Smollett

21. I snatched a cutlass from the pile, and someone, at the same time snatching another, gave me a cut across the knuckles which I hardly felt. - Jim

22. The coast was clear, I made a bolt for it over the stockade and into the thickest of the trees, and before my absence was observed I was out of cry of my companions. - Jim

22. I came to the edge of the retreating water, and wading a little way in, with some strength and dexterity, set my coracle, keel downwards, on the surface. - Jim

23. By good fortune, paddle as I pleased, the tide was still sweeping me down; and there lay the *Hispaniola* right in the fairway, hardly to be missed. - Jim

24. I was on the summit of one swell when the schooner came stooping over the next. The bowsprit was over my head. I sprang to my feet and leaped, stamping the coracle under water. - Jim

25. Come aboard, Mr. Hands. - Jim

25. By the by, I can't have these colours, Mr. Hands; and by your leave, I'll strike 'em. Better none than these. - Jim

25. Now, look here, you gives me food and drink and a old scarf or ankecher to tie my wound up, you do, and I'll tell you how to sail her, and that's about square all round, I take it. - Israel Hands

26. I'll take it kind if you'd step down into that there cabin and get me a—well, a—shiver my timbers! I can't hit the name on 't. - Israel Hands

26. Well, now I tell you, I never seen good come o' goodness yet. Him as strikes first is my fancy; dead men don't bite; them's my views—amen, so be it. - Israel Hands

26. Jim, I reckon we're fouled, you and me, and we'll have to sign articles. I'd have had you but for that there lurch, but I don't have no luck, not I. - Israel Hands

27. With my arms before me I walked steadily in. I should lie down in my own place (I thought with a silent chuckle) and enjoy their faces when they found me in the morning. - Jim

27. Pieces of eight! Pieces of eight! Pieces of eight! Pieces of eight! Pieces of eight! - Captain Flint

28. So, here's Jim Hawkins, shiver my timbers! Dropped in, like, eh? Well, come, I take that friendly. - Long John

28. Well, if I'm to choose, I declare I have a right to know what's what, and why you're here, and where my friends are. - Jim

28. Here you are, in a bad way—ship lost, treasure lost, men lost, your whole business gone to wreck; and if you want to know who did it—it was I! - Jim

29. Look here, now; this ain't lucky! You've gone and cut this out of a Bible. What fool's cut a Bible? - Long John

29. I'm sick to speak to you. You've neither sense nor memory, and I leave it to fancy where your mothers was that let you come to sea. Sea! Gentlemen o' fortune! I reckon tailors is your trade. - Long John

29. So that's the toon, is it? George, I reckon you'll have to wait another turn, friend; and lucky for you as I'm not a revengeful man. - Long John

30. Well, George, how goes it? You're a pretty colour, certainly; why, your liver, man, is upside down. Did you take that medicine? - Dr. Livesey

30. Well, that's done for today. And now I should wish to have a talk with that boy, please. - Dr. Livesey

30. I have blamed myself enough; my life's forfeit anyway, and I should have been dead by now if Silver hadn't stood for me. - Jim

31. Aye, mates, it's lucky you have Barbecue to think for you with this here head. I got what I wanted, I did. - Long John

32. But there's one thing not clear to me. There was an echo. Now, no man ever seen a sperrit with a shadow; well then, what's he doing with an echo to him, I should like to know? - Long John

32. He plucked furiously at the line that held me to him and from time to time turned his eyes upon me with a deadly look. Certainly he took no pains to hide his thoughts, and certainly I read them like print. - Jim

33. So you've changed sides again. - Jim

33. Thank ye kindly, doctor. You came in in about the nick, I guess, for me and Hawkins. And so it's you, Ben Gunn! - Long John

33. John Silver, you're a prodigious villain and imposter—a monstrous imposter, sir. I am told I am not to prosecute you. Well, then, I will not.
- Squire Trelawney

34. Day after day this work went on; by every evening a fortune had been stowed aboard, but there was another fortune waiting for the morrow. - Jim

34. You would lose your precious life, and you may lay to that. I'm on your side now, hand and glove. - Long John

34. The sea-cook had not gone empty-handed. He had cut through a bulkhead unobserved and had removed one of the sacks of coin. - Jim

34. No. You're the man to keep your word, we know that. - Dr. Livesey

34. Of Silver we have heard no more. That formidable seafaring man with one leg has at last gone clean out of my life. - Jim

Treasure Island

Creative Questions and Activities

These options are designed to expand the child's creative and imaginative interaction with the literature. I do not expect every option to be undertaken, and I would like for the child to play a part in choosing the creative activities that he or she will do. If you assign these as written essays, first person is acceptable.

1. Study Long John Silver's pirate words and phrases, and write a poem as Long John, using his quirky language. It can be a funny poem if you like.

2. Jim makes several major decisions on his own, without consulting his friends. Pick one of these solo decisions, imagine that he made a different decision, and explain how that would have changed the plot of the novel.

3. Imagine that Robert Louis Stevenson decided to remove the character of Dr. Livesey from the book and to replace him with a very different person. Create the alternate character, give him a name, and discuss his personality and language. Explain how this changes the story.

4. What is your favorite chapter in *Treasure Island*? Why?

5. You have a terrible, complicated problem in your life, and you can choose one of the characters in *Treasure Island* to come and help you. Who would you choose, and why?

6. Imagine that Stevenson rewrote the ending of *Treasure Island* and that Long John did not slip away but was taken back to Bristol. What happened?

Treasure Island

Academic Writing Practice

Treasure Island provides an excellent basis for academic essay writing. It is filled with advanced language and powerful characters. Robert Louis Stevenson was a serious student of human nature, and his story provides a kind of fictional laboratory where characters are placed in difficult situations, allowing us to watch how they perform. Well-educated children at the middle school and high school levels should find the novel and the following essay questions challenging and appropriate.

In my own courses I use open-book essay questions exclusively as the assessment for literature. I insist that essays be written in standard academic English. They must be true essays, with introductions, bodies, and conclusions centered on single ideas. Students must use the standard conventions of formal style: no contractions, no first person. *Essay Voyage* and my *Advanced Academic Writing* books provide the guidelines for the essays. I like to provide four or five study questions in advance, and I give students several days to prepare for the essays. The actual essay test presents students with three of the study questions, with one being mandatory. Each student chooses one of the remaining two to answer. Making one question mandatory causes students to prepare for all of the study questions, requiring substantial thought and rereading. I do not spring surprise questions on the students. I do believe that some student choice is important.

I provide more than five questions here, and you can select those that you wish to give to the child. You also may replace any of these questions with questions of your own.

These are Socratic questions that do not favor one answer over another; the evaluation of the essays is based on the English, the essay structure, and the force of the case that the child makes with quotations. This means that the child may use his or her book during the essay session in order to quote from it.

---

1. Dr. Livesey and Squire Trelawney make an interesting pair of characters. They have much in common, but they are also very different. Explain how they are different, and then explain why they are friends.

2. Does Jim Hawkins survive the dangers of the story by sheer luck, or does he have qualities and strengths that allow him to survive? Explain.

3. In spite of Long John Silver's obvious reprehensible and repugnant qualities, there is something about him that appeals to us. Even Jim cannot help liking him, and Robert Louis Stevenson is careful to allow Long John to escape unharmed at the end of the story. What is it about Long John that is appealing?

4. Long John Silver's language is very different from Jim Hawkins's language. Is Silver's language distinctive only in vocabulary and phrasing, or is his grammar also different? Explain in detail.

5. Does *Treasure Island* contain insights about life and human behavior, or is it merely an entertaining distraction?

6. Which character changes most in the story: Squire Trelawney or Captain Smollett? What causes the change, and is it for the better?

7. Which character in *Treasure Island* is most admirable? Why?

Treasure Island MLA Paper

As we see in *Advanced Academic Writing, Volume I*, with upper elementary students and higher, we can use the MLA method to write a typed paper about literature. If I were assigning such a paper on *Treasure Island*, I would use it as an opportunity to send the child to the library to become more deeply acquainted with the background of the book and its place in the history of imagination. I would not give the child a thesis but would require him or her to read and reread about Robert Louis Stevenson and about the book and to develop an interesting thesis out of that exploratory reading. That would cause the child to do a great deal of nonfiction reading, thus filling a gap that often exists in the student experience. I would not accept elementary encyclopedias or popular magazines as sources but would have the child explore biographies, literary histories, introductions to various editions of *Treasure Island*, indexes of books about American literature, and any literary encyclopedias that were available.

I would not at this point accept any websites as sources but would use the assignment as an opportunity to show the child what real research is like.

I would assign a three-page MLA paper (depending upon the child's prior writing experience) and would model the assignment on the first paper assignment in *Advanced Academic Writing, Volume I.*

Use this MLA assignment only with children who have studied or are studying *Advanced Academic Writing.*

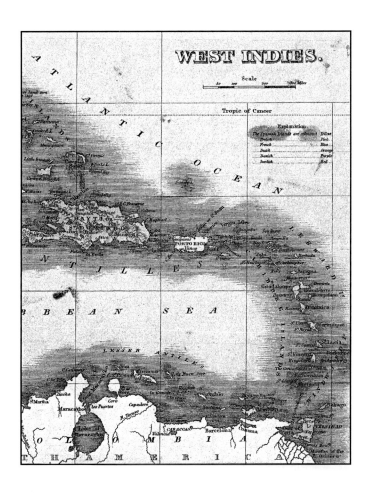

The Call of the Wild

A Comment

To read Jack London is to have the fabric of your thought pervaded by a theme—*theme* is a euphemism for London's disturbing vision of reality—that causes you in gruesome situations for the rest of your life to think, with sober countenance, "This is just like Jack London." You aren't kidding, either. The theme, of course, is the sanguinary instinct of survival—nature red in tooth and claw. Jack London's panoramic display of nature's violence, even the brute thrill of violence, is so vivid that he seems to own the idea, to have invented violence.

London is not subtle about this theme. He clubs us to attention with phrases as brutal as their meaning, calling it "the reign of primitive law," "the heart of things primordial," the "ruthless struggle for existence," Buck's "decivilization," the renewal of "instincts long dead," the "dominant primordial beast," the "articulate travail of existence," the "joy to kill," the "sheer surging of life," the "blood-longing," and the "terrible transformation."

In *The Call of the Wild*, the noun *teeth* appears thirty times, *fang* fifteen times. *Blood* or words containing *blood*, such as *blood-shot*, appears twenty-one times. London might well have titled the book *Red Fang*.

Despite its popularity and prominence as a children's classic, *The Call of the Wild* is no book for the dainty. In chapter after chapter, we wince as people beat dogs, people kill dogs, dogs kill dogs, dogs kill people, and dogs are starved and wounded and blinded and put out of their misery. Blood flies. Bones are broken. Late in the story, Buck stalks a moose in a relentless hunt that seems utterly unredeemed by pity; we excuse the hunting, but the details are a horror.

It is tough to take. Somehow, when I was a boy reading *The Call of the Wild* for the first time, I barely noticed this brutality. The book seemed to be a rousing adventure story that took me to the frozen Northland and gave me a powerful vicarious experience of the chill outdoors, where the carnivorous impulse of nature was a normal expectation. It was cool.

Innocent.

That was six decades ago, and in the interim I

have read history and watched world events unfold, and I now know that human events manifest the call of the wild every bit as much as animal events do. The horrors of World War II alone obviate rash complacency about the progress of civilization. Mark Twain said that history does not repeat itself, but it does rhyme. The rhyme of man's violence against man is a unique cacophony.

The wild is real—and not just in the Northland.

The wild, Pogo would say, is us.

In *The Leviathan*, Thomas Hobbes said that life is "solitary, poor, nasty, brutish, and short."

London, clearly, did not manufacture the idea that nature is violent. Life was violent long before writers wrote about it. Literate tyrannosaurs would have loved Jack London. Nor was London the only author to assign prominence to the red motif. Many classic novels have themes of the cruel inner nature of humanity and the cruelty of the natural world.

Robert Louis Stevenson, let us remember, created not only Long John Silver but also the odious Mr. Hyde, that feral alter ego of Dr. Jekyll who was evil incarnate, a monster who took pleasure in cruelty. In *Lord of the*

Flies, William Golding wrote a fiction-documentary of upper-class British lightfoot lads who, absent the restrictions of civilized culture, degenerate into murder and fell savagery. The holds of right behavior, we see, are tenuous—gossamers of the mind. The red theme also appears in George Orwell's *Animal Farm*, in which power corrupts mercy, and in Mary Shelley's *Frankenstein*, in which the nice people are more cruel to the stitched monster than he is to them. We see the proclivity for cruelty in Stowe's *Uncle Tom's Cabin* and in Victor Hugo's *Les Misérables*. Each title has it own slant on the oft-visited theme, so we should not be shocked to find it in Jack London as well.

But we are.

This book is different.

This book does not feel literary as much as it feels documentary. You read it and *wish* it were fiction.

This book, like Buck's pursuit of the moose, is relentless. It chases us from paragraph to paragraph with its red theme, and it does not stop. Yes, there are moments of kindness, particularly in the relationship between Buck and John Thornton, but these are pulses of text, like punctuation marks, that blip between large expanses of sanguinary chomping.

One might ask how such a menacing book could become a classic—much less a children's classic—of this magnitude, translated into eighty languages and read the world over. Think of that: eighty languages. E. L. Doctorow called London "the most widely read American author in the world." As he was dying, Vladimir Lenin asked his wife to read him a story by Jack London. How could this feral anthem become a global family treasure? Does this story not make readers cry? Are there not children who put the book down and refuse to read another page?

I think that there are, but not as many as one would expect.

This book gets read. It is an odium that we cannot hate. For many readers, including young readers, *The Call of the Wild* is their favorite book. There is something about it, a toothy *je ne sais quoi*.

After all of the slaughter, we find ourselves cheering for Buck, never mind that his path is a steady descent (Is it an ascent?) from civilization to hirsute brutality. We cheer for Buck, I think, because of the way he sorts through his options, being open to kindness and the love of John Thornton but rising to grim peril with grimmer courage—every time—and doing what he must to survive. Buck fights back, and we like it.

No quitter is Buck.

To paraphrase Robert Frost, something there is that doesn't love a quitter. In a sense, Buck's story is an allegory for the can-do American experience, of dealing with the wild, of overcoming, of solving our problems without help from anyone, of doing what we must, of improvising and fighting and forging life out of chaos.

Buck personifies our yearning to fight back.

Dogifies is not a word.

Buck, of course, does not conquer the wild; he amalgamates with it. He becomes one with the One. This is an allegory in reverse. It is by becoming wild that Buck survives the wild. He accepts the call. He embraces the call. He takes himself out of conflict with it. A guerilla character, he fades into the red world, becoming one with it. He wills himself to be absorbed.

By the time you realize that *The Call of the Wild* is not really a dog book, that Buck is too anthropomorphized to be doggy, that, like Cassius, Buck thinks too much, that Buck is merely a pronoun swapped for the noun of human beings, that the real theme is the wild side of *human* nature, it is too late. You already have read the story and faced its premise before you have put up your defenses and rationalizations. The dog part was London's smokescreen, his subterfuge, his writer's feint. The book itself is our call of the wild; it is its red theme that grips us to the pages, that will not let us look away.

For all of our dreams and idealism, for all of humanity's genuinely admirable and civilized accomplishments, there is the inexorable red theme blinking in the trees that requires our awareness. History does not lie. In intellectual honesty, for the sake of clarity, we cannot take a Pollyannaish approach to reality. We might thrill to the words of Browning's, "All's right with the world," but we are brought back by Hemingway's final words in *The Sun Also Rises*: "Isn't it pretty to think so?"

Buck's story helps us keep our thinking in balance.

The Call of the Wild

Language Illustration Questions

1. Please read all of the language illustrations in Chapter 1 and explain what, as a group, they show you about Jack London's writing style.

2. The language illustration on page 35 has to do with vowels, and the language illustration on page 52 has to do with consonants. Which of the two do you think is most interesting? Why?

3. Please study the language illustration on page 68 and think about why a passage about blood would emphasize the consonant *l*. Why would *l* be more effective for this purpose than, say, an *m* or an *s*?

4. What is the point of the language illustration on page 81? What does this show you about writing strategy? Also, please examine the language

illustration on page 83; does this illustration surprise you? Why? Which of these two language illustrations is more important? Explain.

5.   Which of the language illustrations in Chapter 6 is most interesting to you? Why?

6.   Do you think that all of the language illustrations in Chapter 7 are really making the same point? Why or why not?

7.   Which two language illustrations in this novel are most important? Explain.

8.   Select a language illustration that impresses you because it shows how effective London's technique could be. In other words, what is an example of one of London's techniques that worked brilliantly?

The Call of the Wild
Character Quotations for Quote Quizzes

We cannot use typical quote quizzes for *The Call of the Wild*, chiefly because the main character is a dog who never says a sentence. Accordingly, if the passage is a quotation spoken by a character, then the child must identify whose words those are, but if the passage is a narrative description of a character, then the child should identify who is described.

1. He plunged into the swimming tank or went hunting with the Judge's sons. - Buck

1. He had one besetting sin. He loved to play Chinese lottery. Also, in his gambling, he had one besetting weakness—faith in a system. - Manuel

1. He had learned to trust in men he knew, and to give them credit for a wisdom that outreached his own. - Buck

1. Now, you red-eyed devil. - man in red sweater

1. Well, Buck, my boy, we've had our little ruction, and the best thing we can do is to let it go at that. You've learned your place, and I know mine. Be a good dog and all 'll go well and the goose hang high. Be a bad dog, and I'll whale the stuffin' outa you. - man in red sweater

1. He was friendly, in a treacherous sort of way, smiling into one's face while he meditated some underhand trick, as, for instance, when he stole from Buck's food at the first meal. - Spitz

2. He ran out his tongue and laughed again, and from that moment Buck hated him with a bitter and deathless hatred. - Spitz

2. He had one peculiarity which Buck was unlucky enough to discover. He did not like to be approached on his blind side. - Sol-leks

2. And with a ferocious snarl he bounded straight up into the blinding day, the snow flying about him in a flashing cloud. - Buck

2. As courier for the Canadian Government, bearing important despatches, he was anxious to secure the best dogs, and he was particularly gladdened by the possession of Buck. - Perrault

2. This first theft marked him as fit to survive in the hostile Northland environment. It marked his adaptability, his capacity to adjust himself to changing conditions, the lack of which would have meant swift and terrible death. - Buck

3. A-a-ah! Gif it to heem, by Gar! Gif it to heem, the dirty t'eef! - Francois

3. He was a practised fighter. From Spitzbergen through the Arctic, and across Canada and the Barrens, he had held his own with all manner of dogs and achieved to mastery over them. Bitter rage was his, but never blind rage. - Spitz

3. But he possessed a quality that made for greatness—imagination. He fought by instinct, but he could fight by head as well. He rushed, as though attempting the old shoulder trick, but at the last instant swept low to the snow and in. - Buck

4. But he was in open revolt. He wanted, not to escape a clubbing, but to have the leadership. It was his by right. He had earned it, and he would not be content with less. - Buck

4. Nevaire such a dog as dat Buck! No, nevaire! Heem worth one t'ousan' dollair. - Francois

4. Sometimes he thought of Judge Miller's big house in the sun-kissed Santa Clara Valley, and of the cement swimming-tank, and Ysabel, the Mexican hairless. - Buck

4. So he was harnessed in again, and proudly he pulled as of old, though more than once he cried out involuntarily from the bite of his inward hurt.

Several times he fell down and was dragged in the traces. - Dave

5. Oh, Hal, you mustn't. The poor dears! Now you must promise you won't be harsh with them for the rest of the trip, or I won't go a step. - Mercedes

5. He felt vaguely that there was no depending upon these two men and the woman. They did not know how to do anything, and as the days went by it became apparent that they could not learn. - Buck

5. She no longer considered the dogs, and because she was sore and tired, she persisted in riding on the sled. - Mercedes

5. And they told you true. The bottom's likely to drop out at any moment. Only fools, with the blind luck of fools, could have made it. I tell you straight, I wouldn't risk my carcass on that ice for all the gold in Alaska. - John Thornton

---

5.   If you strike that dog again, I'll kill you.
     - John Thornton

6.   He was a thing of the wild, come in from the wild
     to sit by John Thornton's fire, rather than a dog
     of the soft Southland stamped with the marks of
     generations of civilization. - Buck

6.   As Buck struck him like a battering ram, with the
     whole force of the current behind him, he reached
     up and closed with both arms around the shaggy
     neck. - John Thornton

6.   Can you lend me a thousand? - John Thornton

7.   He asked little of man or nature. He was unafraid
     of the wild. With a handful of salt and a rifle he
     could plunge into the wilderness and fare wherever
     he pleased and as long as he pleased.
     - John Thornton

7. But especially he loved to run in the dim twilight of the summer midnights, listening to the subdued and sleepy murmurs of the forest, reading signs and sounds as man may read a book. - Buck

7. After some time of this he started off at an easy lope in a manner that plainly showed he was going somewhere. He made it clear to Buck that he was to come. - the wolf

7. From his St. Bernard father he had inherited size and weight, but it was his shepherd mother who had given shape to that size and weight. His muzzle was the long wolf muzzle, save that it was larger than the muzzle of any wolf. - Buck

7. They scattered far and wide over the country, and it was not till a week later that the last of the survivors gathered together in a lower valley and counted their losses. - the Yeehats

The Call of the Wild
Creative Questions and Activities

1. What character in *Treasure Island* is most like John Thornton? Why? Or: Who in *Treasure Island* most reminds you of Hal, Charles, and Mercedes?

2. Imagine that Long John Silver arrives at Buck's Northland, and he enters one of the scenes that is in *The Call of the Wild*. What happens?

3. Would you rather have John Thornton or Dr. Livesey as a neighbor? Why?

4. In an old box in a university library, you have discovered a lost chapter of *The Call of the Wild*, one that Jack London intended to include. What happens in the discovered chapter?

5. What would Long John Silver think of John Thornton?

The Call of the Wild

Academic Writing Practice

Here are open-ended study questions about *The Call of the Wild* and *Treasure Island*. These are academic questions that will give the child practice writing academic essays with formal style and content.

Give the child four or five questions to study, pick three of those for writing practice or an essay test, and make one mandatory. The child writes the mandatory essay and one other. Quotations from the text to prove a case are required.

At least one of the final three questions should be a cumulative question that includes both *The Call of the Wild* and *Treasure Island*.

You might enjoy discussing these questions before narrowing down to study questions.

For a younger child, use the questions as the basis of fun discussions, and let the child pick a question to write about, using *Paragraph Town* or *Essay Voyage* as a guide.

For an older child, use *Essay Voyage* or *Advanced Academic Writing* as a guide.

1. In *The Call of the Wild*, Buck goes through a transition from being a pampered family dog to being a dominant wild animal. Is there a moment that is the main turning point in Buck's transition?

2. What three passages in *The Call of the Wild* best express the novel's central theme?

3. What major moment in *The Call of the Wild* is most similar to a major moment in *Treasure Island*?

4. Which novel has the most realistic characters: *The Call of the Wild* or *Treasure Island*?

5. Every novel is in some sense a portrait of reality. Do *The Call of the Wild* and *Treasure Island* present similar images of reality or opposing images? We are not talking here about realistic descriptions of nature and beings, but of the real nature of the world, the meaning of the world.

6. We cannot say that Buck was completely forced to the wild position he reached at the end of the novel. To some extent, he had a choice. At what point might he have made a choice that would have led him back to a tame life?

7. Even though Buck is a dog, he has an awareness that is strikingly human. He notices things, he likes and dislikes things, he has feelings. What character in *Treasure Island* is most like Buck?

8. Who is more of a survivor: Buck or Long John Silver?

9. Considering all of the characters in *The Call of the Wild* and *Treasure Island*, which one is the most admirable?

The Call of the Wild MLA Paper

For older children: We now have read both *Treasure Island* and *The Call of the Wild*, two novels in which characters are placed in dangerous worlds and have to survive with their character and intelligence. These novels present the more advanced student with an opportunity to write a paper comparing and/or contrasting them.

A three-page MLA paper is not long enough to accommodate all of the similarities and distinctions of the two books, so the child will have to reread, think, and find one interesting element that can be compared and/or contrasted.

This paper is a literary think-piece, using quotations from both novels, rather than a research paper that introduces quotations from external research. For a detailed explanation of this method, see *Advanced Academic Writing, Volume I.*

The Invisible Man

A Comment

Your first thought, of course, is that it would be cool to be invisible. There, I said it. *Cool.* Cool in the dictionary sense of "fashionably impressive or excellent." Can there be anyone in the world who has not wished, at one time or another, to be invisible, or to be able to be at times?

Why? That is the question.

Why would we want invisibility?

What would we do, unseen, that we would not do if seen? We want to be invisible because....

"I wish I could be," we sometimes say, "a fly on the wall." It is essentially the same wish—to be present but unseen. Typically, one imagines, the motive is social espionage. We want to know what *they* say about us when we are not around. The social espionage motive is probably universal; we all wish we knew what they say, even though it might mortify us.

In *Treasure Island*, young master Hawkins experiences a fly-on-the-wall moment, and in it he learns exactly what the pirates say when he is not present. Jim listens from the apple barrel as the pirates discuss mutiny and murder, with himself included in the victim list. Hiding in the barrel, inches from the conniving blackguards, Jim is not physically invisible, but he is present and unseen. He hears what the pirates say in his putative absence and learns that their private words contradict their effusive public hypocrisies of affection and fidelity. Jim's situation is the opportunity of a moment only, and we do not see him abuse the advantage that he gains from eavesdropping. He simply reports the pirate perfidies to his friends.

The question of invisibility is revealing, H.G. Wells shows us in *The Invisible Man*, because it concerns the moral choices of the individual in the absence of social and cultural monitors. Invisibility makes it possible to detach oneself from social mores—indeed, from social observation. With invisibility, the burden of morality falls to the individual. If an individual could be invisible at will, would he or she use that power for right actions? Would will become ill will?

It is commonly thought that Jack London was influenced by Nietzsche and that London's novels depict a will-to-power über-individualism, but even Jack London differentiated himself from that steel purity, explaining that his view of the matter involved more altruism. H.G. Wells's Invisible Man does not thus waver. He moves steadily and without noticeable trepidations toward a serene, morally hollow, almost sociopathic collection of solutions. The moral status of these solutions plays little part in his thought.

"It isn't wrong," one of my students once said, "if you don't get caught." After I picked myself up off of the floor, we had a frank and useful class discussion. His callow position accorded with what Kohlberg would have called *preconventional* morality, the state in which you do the right thing only under threat, only to avoid being punished. The antithesis of this position is what Kohlberg called *postconventional* morality, in which you develop your moral maturity to the point that you do the right thing because you believe, because you have internalized the beauty and clarity of moral thought; you have both seen and felt the light, and it is now your sincerest care to do right things.

In postconventional morality, you do the right thing whether you are seen or not, whether you are alone or not, whether you will be rewarded or punished or not, and your moral allegiance is to the big SG, to Something Greater than yourself or even than your society. In religious terms, you do it God's way. Postconventional moral individuals will do the right thing even if they are punished—or even killed—for doing so, as the great martyrs of civilization plainly document. In this regard we think, for example, of German citizens who sheltered Jewish neighbors during the Nazi horror, risking their lives to do so. We think of Antigone defying the orders of King Creon and burying her brother. Martin Luther is reported to have said, "Here I stand, I can do no other." For an individual of postconventional moral feeling, the right action is the only imaginable course; there is no other, and knowingly to do wrong would be an emotional impossibility.

Give me morality, one might say, or give me death.

One fictional case of postconventional morality is found in E.M. Forster's *A Passage to India*, in which Mrs. Moore, an English woman, enters a Hindu shrine in the darkness of night. Dr. Aziz, a physician, sees her enter the shrine and accosts her with the admonition that she must not be there with her shoes on:

"Madam, this is a mosque, you have no right here at all; you should have taken off your shoes; this is a holy place for Moslems."

"I have taken them off."

"You have?"

"I left them at the entrance."

"Then I ask your pardon."

Still startled, the woman moved out, keeping the ablution-tank between them. He called after her, "I am truly sorry for speaking."

"Yes, I was right, was I not? If I remove my shoes, I am allowed?"

"Of course, but so few ladies take the trouble, especially if thinking no one is there to see."

"That makes no difference. God is here."

For English Mrs. Moore, God is everywhere, and right action is obligatory, and it matters not whether she is alone, or invisible, or caught. Even when no other person is here, God is always here, and one is never invisible to God, and one's misdeeds are always watched. The eye of God sees every sin, every crime. Wherever you are, there is God, too. Keeping it simple, Mrs. Moore does it by the Book: she does unto this holy shrine as she would have anyone in the world do to her holy shrine. The fact that this shrine is holy to a religion different from her own is irrelevant. She would not wish a Moslem to desecrate her church, and in accordance with the Biblical injunction, she would not wish to desecrate a Moslem shrine.

Mrs. Moore's moral imperative would be an incomprehensible anomaly in Jack London's Northland. It would signify a fatal weakness. In Buck's world, survival is the right action; to hesitate is to die, to shrink is to die, and we do not see—in any character—a shred of desire to die for a cause. Survival of self is the dominant impulse, and it is pursued by any means necessary. Though nominally a dog, Buck devolves through a series of human-like moral stages, eventually reaching an absolute acceptance of the law of the wild and everything that it entails. Buck becomes ferocity incarnate.

Then there is Griffin, Wells's Invisible Man, who inhabits a complicated and shifting moral locus somewhere at a midpoint in the continuum between Mrs. Moore and Buck. No Mrs. Moore is he.

Like the mythical, treasure-guarding griffin that is a combination of an eagle and a lion, Griffin is powerful but complex, shifting from genius and nobility in one moment to cruelty and egocentrism the next. Even as his grip on civilized mores slips from his heart, he still dreams of continuing his research, still looks toward the light of scientific inquiry. He has albino characteristics, and these may have contributed to his lifelong feeling of isolation, and that may have weakened the reins of proscription that hold ordinary people in check.

Like Buck, Griffin finds himself in extreme isolation, without any of the normal support systems that make life amenable or survival reasonable. Like Buck, Griffin resorts increasingly to acts of crime and violence to navigate the perils of his condition, and like Buck, he feels increasingly comfortable with that.

In the end the theme of the book inverts; instead of adopting the cold theme as our mantra, we become sickened by it and understand, better than before, what we really care about.

When we close the cover of *The Invisible Man*, we feel, to our surprise, relieved that we are not invisible. It is not merely that we do not wish to suffer the myriad hassles of invisibility and the social isolation that invisibility imposes; it is that we become more conscious of our conscience, that we realize that we do not want to scrape at the margins of moral decision, having to invent our own rules for right action and being tempted to do things we will regret. By placing Griffin in the unforgiving laboratory of fiction, Wells has shown us that for all of its problems and hypocrisies, civilization is, after all, civilized, and it is better to be visible.

The Invisible Man

Language Illustration Questions

1. Please study the language illustration on page 14. What difference does it make whether a structure is parallel or not? Why do great writers go to the trouble of writing parallel structures?

2. Which two language illustrations in Chapters 1-5 do you think are most interesting? Why?

3. What is the point of the language illustration on page 103?

4. Please study the language illustration on page 111 and explain the point of Wells's technique.

5. Please review the language illustrations in Chapters 1-20 and select the two that you think demonstrate the most powerful poetic technique.

6.   What do you think of the simile described in the language illustration on page 234? Is it effective?

7.   Please explain what you learned about passive voice verbs on page 250.

8.   What is the best language illustration in Chapters 25-28? Why?

9.   If you were going to pick three language illustrations from this novel to show to friends to teach them some of the secrets of great writing, which three would you choose? Please explain why you chose each one.

The Invisible Man

Character Quotations for Quote Quizzes

Not every chapter is represented by quotations. Some chapters are narrative only, and others are short and have no quotations that are suitable.

1. A fire, in the name of human charity! A room and a fire! - Griffin (Invisible Man)

1. The poor soul's had an accident or an op'ration or somethin'. What a turn them bandages did give me, to be sure! - Mrs. Hall

2. My eyes—are sometimes so weak and painful that I have to shut myself up in the dark for hours together. - Griffin

2. Why don't you finish and go? All you've got to do is to fix the hour-hand on its axle. - Griffin

3. The sooner you get those things in the better I'll be pleased. - Griffin

3. Certainly, sir. You can turn the lock if you're like that, you know. Any time. - Mrs. Hall

4. He may be a bit overbearing, but bills settled punctual is bills settled punctual, whatever you'd like to say. - Mrs. Hall

4. No hand—just an empty sleeve. Lord! I thought, that's a deformity! Got a cork arm, I suppose, and has taken it off. - Mr. Cuss

5. The candle! Who lit the candle? - Mr. Bunting

6. If 'e en't there, 'is close are. And what's 'e doin' 'ithout 'is close, then? 'Tas a most curious business. - Mr. Hall

6. Lock him out. Don't let him come in again. I half guessed—I might ha' known. With them goggling

eyes and bandaged head, and never going to church of a Sunday. - Mrs. Hall

7. Why wasn't my breakfast laid? Why haven't you prepared my meals and answered my bell? Do you think I live without eating? - Griffin

7. I told you two days ago I wasn't going to await no remittances. You can't grumble if your breakfast waits a bit, if my bill's been waiting these five days, can you? - Mrs. Hall

9. It's a beast of a country. And pigs for people. - Griffin

9. I'm—off—my—blooming—chump. It's no good. It's fretting about them blarsted boots. I'm off my blessed blooming chump. Or it's spirits. - Marvel

9. You 'aven't been eatin' bread and cheese? - Marvel

11. I'd rather glance through the volumes first. A general impression first, Cuss, and then, you know, we can go looking for clues. - Mr. Bunting

11. It's incredible, incredible. But the fact remains that I saw—I certainly saw right down his sleeve. - Mr. Cuss

13. It's bad enough to let these floundering yokels explode my little secret, without your cutting off with my books. It's lucky for some of them they cut and ran when they did! - Griffin

13. Oh! shut up! I'll see to you all right. You do what you're told. You'll do it all right. You're a fool and all that, but you'll do— - Griffin

14. He didn't have any pals—it don't say he had any pals, does it? - Marvel

14. Suppose he wants to rob—who can prevent him? He can trespass, he can burgle, he could walk through a cordon of policemen as easy as me or you could give the slip to a blind man! - mariner

15. "'Visible Man a-coming, sir!" I can't imagine what possesses people. One might think we were in the thirteenth century. - Kemp

16. Lemme go inside. Lock me in—somewhere. I tell you he's after me. I give him the slip. He said he'd kill me and he will. - Marvel

17. A younger student than you were, almost an albino, six feet high, and broad, with a pink and white face and red eyes, who won the medal for chemistry. - Griffin

17. But how was it all done? And how did you get like this? - Kemp

18. Is there such a thing as an invisible animal? In the sea, yes. Thousands—millions. All the larvae, all the little nauplii and tornarias, all the microscopic things, the jelly-fish. In the sea there are more things invisible than visible! - Kemp

18. He's not only invisible, but he's mad! Homicidal! - Kemp

19. I went there after I left London. You know I dropped medicine and took up physics? No; well, I did. Light fascinated me. - Griffin

19. Either a body absorbs light, or it reflects or refracts it, or does all these things. If it neither reflects nor refracts nor absorbs light, it cannot of itself be visible. - Griffin

19. And I, a shabby, poverty-struck, hemmed-in demonstrator, teaching fools in a provincial college, might suddenly become—this. - Griffin

20. For the most part, saving certain gaps I chose to remember, they are written in cypher in those books that tramp has hidden. We must hunt him down. We must get those books again. - Griffin

20. It was alive four days after, I know, and down a grating in Great Titchfield Street; because I saw a crowd round the place, trying to see whence the miaowing came. - Griffin

20. It's the devil. It's the palaeolithic in a bottle. - Kemp

21. I looked down and saw the youngsters had stopped and were gaping at the muddy footmarks I had left behind me up the newly whitened steps. - Griffin

22. Silence came upon the place, and I found myself wandering through the vast and intricate shops, galleries, show-rooms of the place, alone. - Griffin

23. Knocked him on the head? - Kemp

23. But still, in England—to-day. And the man was in his own house, and you were—well, robbing. - Kemp

23. And he made me wild too—hunting me about the house, fooling about with his revolver, locking and unlocking doors. He was simply exasperating. You don't blame me, do you? You don't blame me?
- Griffin

24. He's in the town police station, locked up, by his own request, in the strongest cell in the place.
- Kemp

24. Blundering into your house changes all my plans. For you are a man that can understand. - Griffin

24. We have to consider all that invisibility means, all that it does not mean. It means little advantage for eavesdropping and so forth—one makes sounds.
- Griffin

25. He is pure selfishness. He thinks of nothing but his own advantage, his own safety. I have listened to such a story this morning of brutal self-seeking.
- Kemp

---

27.   We will have him! And I am the bait. He will come too far. - Kemp

27.   I have it!   Let me have a stick or something, and I'll go down to the station and get the bloodhounds put on. That ought to settle him! - Adye

27.   You go back to the house. I tell you flatly I will not promise anything. - Griffin

28.   Get back, you fools! He's hurt, I tell you. Stand back! - Kemp

The Invisible Man

Creative Questions and Activities

1. Who would be more capable of dealing with the Invisible Man (Griffin): John Thornton from *The Call of the Wild* or Long John Silver from *Treasure Island*?

2. *The Invisible Man* comes to a terrible end. Could that have been avoided? What plot twist might H.G. Wells have used that would have led to a happy ending?

3. Think of an important idea on which the Invisible Man and Long John Silver would agree.

4. Imagine that the Invisible Man was on Treasure Island when the *Hispaniola* arrived. Would he have joined the pirates, or would he have joined Jim and his friends? Why?

The Invisible Man

Academic Writing Practice

Here are open-ended study questions about *Treasure Island*, *The Call of the Wild*, and *The Invisible Man*. For younger children, these questions can be a source of fun discussions and of introductory-level academic writing. For advanced students, give the child four or five questions to study, pick three of those for the test, and make one mandatory. The child writes the mandatory essay and one other. Quotations from the text to prove a case are required.

At least one of the final three questions should be a cumulative question that includes all three novels.

You might enjoy discussing these questions with the child before narrowing down to five study questions. The child might enjoy having some choice; perhaps he or she could choose two of the questions.

1. Does Griffin have a worthwhile scientific reason for developing invisibility? Does he make any attempt to do anything valuable with the discovery?

2. Thomas Marvel plays a significant part in the plot of *The Invisible Man*. Are Marvel's actions and decisions reasonable and appropriate, given the situation he faces, or does he blunder?

3. Griffin appears to be utterly isolated in *The Invisible Man*. Even his relationship with Kemp never rises to what we would call friendship. Does Griffin's invisibility explain his isolation, or does he have other characteristics that would make him isolated in any case?

4. Does Jack London's character Buck have qualities that would have helped Griffin survive?

5. Who is least admirable: Griffin or Long John Silver?

---

6. Which novel presents the most reassuring view of the world: *Treasure Island*, *The Call of the Wild*, or *The Invisible Man*?

7. Can you see a significant theme that is present in all three novels?

8. Which novel has the most poetic writing in it: *Treasure Island*, *The Call of the Wild*, or *The Invisible Man*?

9. Which of the three novels has the most to teach us about living a good and moral life: *Treasure Island*, *The Call of the Wild*, or *The Invisible Man*?

10. Considering *Treasure Island*, *The Call of the Wild*, and *The Invisible Man*, which novel has the best developed and most memorable character?

The Invisible Man MLA Paper

Treasure Island, *The Call of the Wild*, and *The Invisible Man* focus almost exclusively on male characters. Female characters are few, and they play minor roles in the plots. We see Jim's mother in *Treasure Island*, Mercedes in *The Call of the Wild*, and Mrs. Hall in *The Invisible Man*.

A too-political or propaganda-level explanation of the novels would probably oversimplify the situation. It would be too simple, for example, to say that these female characters are all negative portrayals of women. Of the three, Mercedes is starkly weaker than the other two, who both show signs of an independent mind and courage in dangerous situations. Jim Hawkins's mother, particularly, appears willing to stand up for herself.

Furthermore, as human beings the novelists were exceptionally diverse. They were not three alpha males, pounding their chests. It would be difficult to find three more different writers than Stevenson, London, and Wells. Stevenson was thin and sickly, London was rough and tumble, and Wells was a British sophisticate.

It is true that none of them was a conventional person, but then writers rarely are, and these three were artistic, idiosyncratic, and eccentric. We do not see salient signs of misogyny in the biographies of the three writers.

What we do see is a common love of writing.

History and culture likely play some part in the explanation. The three novels were published within twenty years of each other: *Treasure Island* first in 1883, then *The Invisible Man* in 1897, and then *The Call of the Wild* in 1903, seventeen years before the Nineteenth Amendment gave women the right to vote in the United States on August 18, 1920.

Still, it is curious that all three novels share this imbalance regarding male characters. After all, Jane Austen had written *Pride and Prejudice* in 1813, and Charlotte Brontë had published *Jane Eyre* in 1847. For that matter, Shakespeare had given us strong female characters as far back as *Julius Caesar*, and Sir Walter Scott gave us strong female characters in his brilliant *Ivanhoe*, published in 1820, so it is not that strong female characters were unheard of when Stevenson, London, and Wells were writing.

We do, by the way, see modern novels that have a

similar cast of characters, such as William Golding's *Lord of the Flies*. No girls there.

So what are we to make of the concentration of male characters? Is it simply a coincidence, an accident of choice that connects the three novels, or is there something that should be discussed?

Using the guidelines delineated in the *Advanced Academic Writing* series, write a paper exploring the underrepresentation of female characters in these three novels.

Your reading will give you ideas for your paper, but you might reread the passages involving the three women, looking for common characteristics in the way they were portrayed.